Copyright ©2021 by Mark A. Green and Diane Nemea Laessig

All rights reserved. This book or any portion thereof may not be reproduced or used in any manner whatsoever without the express written permission of the publisher except for the use of brief quotations in a book review or scholarly journal.

Second Printing: 2023

ISBN 978-0-578-83274-6

Green Dragon Publishing
1818 Primavera Ct.
Santa Rosa, CA 95409

Ordering Information:
Special discounts are available on quantity purchases by corporations, associations, educators, and others. For details, contact the publisher at the above listed address.
U.S. trade bookstores and wholesalers: Please contact Green Dragon Publishing at sonomamark@comcast.net.

A Red Kiss

Selected Poems 1993-2020

Mark A. Green

Photography by Diane Nemea Laessig

Green Dragon Publishing

2021

FOREWORD

Poetry comes to me in moments.

These poems arrived like fleeting glimpses into a world of revelations and kindness, a place inside myself where a glowing, liminal space opens to embrace the world both as it is and as it could be. Even those written in pain, I suppose, could be considered hopeful, aspiring to transcendence and comprehension of the struggles we face as humans.

I am grateful for the journey, for all its lumps and bumps, and to the many friends and beloved ones who have contributed to the moments that birthed these works.

—Mark Green

INVOKING A BOOK
(A Spell)

Bathe with vervain.
Walk naked, counting
Thirteen steps thirteen more
Cool feet padding to the circle place
And turn three times around. Place

A pinch of dried oak leaves, there on the brazier,
Soft plumes of sweet autumn's scent
And the memory of a forest. A tiny bead of dragon's blood
For Mystery, and just perhaps
Frankincense, to call what threadbare gods there
may be left.

Now, the cauldron.
Odd, for such peculiar art, no liquid is defined: only
double
And bubble, and herbs resembling creature bits

But *we* know: *wine*,
Alchemy of soil and rain and sun gone stiff
And wild in the barrel. Pour it and brew, fume rising and
Stir, saying
Earth Air Water
Fire burn and cauldron bubble
Add, then, the Particular Things: a twig, a button,
Salt and oil of cedar: so.
Place left hand on your sex

Whisper the Wish three times and
Stir, saying
Earth and Sky
Let it be so Let it be so
Let cool.
Tomorrow you will
Pour into cool, dark earth, saying
It is finished It is finished
It is magic it is done.

Repeat.

Contents

Foreword	1
Invoking a Book (A Spell)	2
LOVE SONGS	7
Atheists Prayer	8
Another Love Poem	10
Blessed	11
A Far Country	12
Mary Magdalene Impenitent	14
Morning Prayer	16
Millennials	18
Falling Through	19
The Very Word	20
Years After	21
Troll	22
Dea Gratias	23
STRUGGLES AND SORROWS	25
12/5/93: Taking the Flyer Down	26
DEPRESSION—A Cycle	27
The Avalanche	33
Varicella	34
THE WHEEL OF THE YEAR	37
Mulled Wine (Yule)	38
Three Percent (Riverain/Imbolc/Brightening)	39

Spring Laughs (High Spring)	40
May Morning (May Day)	41
Dawn Prayer (Midsummer)	42
Gifts of a Problem Sabbath (Dimming)	43
The Crush (Harvest)	44
In Memoriam Solis Victi (Autumn)	45
Mystery (Hallows)	46
Vigil	50

Love Songs

AN ATHEIST'S PRAYER

Praise to the wide spinning world
Unfolding each of all the destined tales compressed
In the moment of your catastrophic birth
Wide to the fluid expanse, blowing outward
Kindling in stars and galaxies, in bright pools
Of Christmas-colored gas; cohering in marbles hot
And cold, ringed, round, gray and red and gold and dun

And blue

Pure blue, the eye of a child, spinning in a veil of air,
Warm island, home to us, kind beyond measure: the stones
And trees, the round river flowing sky to deepest chasm, salt
And sweet.

Praise to Time, enormous and precious,
And we with so little, seeing our world go as it will
Ruing, cheering, the treasured fading, precious arriving,
Fear and wonder,
Fear and wonder always.

Praise O black expanse of mostly nothing
Though you do not hear, you have no ear nor mind to hear
Praise O inevitable, O mysterious, praise
Praise and thanks be a wave

Expanding from this tiny temporary mouth this tiny dot
Of world a bubble

Going out forever meeting everything as it goes
All the great and infinitesimal
Gracious and terrible
All the works of blessed Being.

May it be so.

May it be so.

May our hearts sing to say it is so.

ANOTHER LOVE POEM

Sonoma I will drink the drift
Of all your dust and memory
Forever: knock back whiskey on
A creaky Occidental porch; recount
The families who name the vineland roads:
These came from Missouri, those
Climbed Donner Pass.

Sonoma I am sifting grates of your memory, sniffing
Captured wisps of redwood fog in August,
Gulping lemon tarweed air speaking
Your generosity. Between the coming freeway
Lanes, the tracks of wagons linger,

Sledges too. Sonoma I will not forget.
The Russians will not let me, they are
Shouting clad in beaver skins.
The Pomo will not let me, they
Are pounding acorn meats to mush.

The oaks will not let me
They are dancing down the meadows to the sea.

BLESSED

For my people—you know who you are

I am among the blessed.

I am of the kind who leaves the glaring tube, remembering
And goes to watch the moon rise silver through the trees
Breathing purple and chill, stinging pine. I am
Among the blessed: I know the acacia, the first daffodil,
The irises unsheathing cream and violet labia in the green wet of
                                                                                                   May.
I tune for the new music on the radio: I turn it up.

I am among the blessed: I drink wine by firelight, clothes rank
                                                                                                    with smoke,
Bright silver twisted through my lobes. I know secrets;
They are tattooed on my body where the sleeves can cover them,
They read

Blessed, and only if we are lucky enough, you and I, courageous
                                                                                                    enough
To shed our clothes together will you read them.

Seeing scarlet leaves drift down,
Perhaps, with ice around the moon, or the steel bones of the oaks
                                                                                               against Orion,
Knowing we are among the blessed, that we miss nothing, that
we will eat this life
Like a chocolate mango, like Beethoven ice cream,
Moaning our joy with each sweet bite.

A FAR COUNTRY
For Ellen Lewis

It comes in moments, thinking:
Oh, that year is still out there somewhere. We could drive
Far into the night and come upon it,
A world of remembered fashions and faded devices.

But then your bones confirm: no.
Those days are gone for always, lost
In the strangeness that is the passing of time.
We are older now.

Remembering, there is always the will to bring
What has been gained on this roadworn way back
On that trip: strapped to the roof like campers' gear,
Waiting to unfurl and make a new home.

We would have our wisdom and our youth besides then.
No aches and infirmities, and optimism bright as peaches,
Innocence without inexperience. We would have all
We have won by endurance, and cost free.

The far land of the past would take us then, unmake
The failures and embarrassments, take
The work and sorrow from us, the mistakes,
Leaving gold, and we young and beautiful to spend it.

Oh, if it were only so.

But we are not passengers--nor drivers, really:
We calve like ice from floes laid down in bygone snows
Jagged and dangerous, mostly unseen
And float down the currents, rounding
Softening
Learning our depths as we diminish until
Blue with history, curved and scalloped
With knowing this great ocean at last
We are melted into the vastness of things.

MARY MAGDALENE IMPENITENT

And so I have become an object lesson to these old, dried men.
A cautionary tale. They know nothing, these friends,
                                    these hangers-on,
They have only their dreams of what was given them,
                                    the longed-for balm,
Freedom from their secret lusts as seen
In the mirror he was for each he met,
As Pilate did. And I.

What they do not tell you in their book fills chests of scrolls
In the library of my heart, will die with me. His sorrow, his rage,
                                    his agony
They embrace, they exalt, the old men who think this fire in their
                                    eyes is his
—When it is their own—
But his sweetness, his passion, his humanity they choose
                                    to forget, confounded
That a whore held his confidences, that we shared what
                                    they could not,
Who would consume him, tear him to pieces and eat him
                                    to have what he was.

Who will tell that his skin smelled of honey in the sun? That his
                                    mouth was red
As berries, filled with juices, alive on me, how long his
                                    fingers were, and gentle,

How his back arched when he spilled into me? Who will
                              say that he laughed often,
And at little things? That he snored? Loved figs and
                                        pomegranates,
But did not care for dates?
Who will remember his fear, his questioning?

I cursed the corrupt old men when they took him from me.
I cursed God.

And I repent nothing. Not even this.

MORNING PRAYER

Celebrate the self that chimes, and bring
A hand of unexpected ice-cream
Down between the plumbing traps and cleansers
Where the self that's hiding cries
And listen for the dark arrangement
Out on bare earth cracked with stamping
Of bitter feet, and don't reject
But just reshoe them, and let them go.

Celebrate the self that chimes, when
The rind's gone in with the juice
With three letters written, and only one stamp,
And the day burns on, innocent of lists and plans
And find the one, perfect thorn, and say,
"<u>This</u> is my aliveness"; let its sharpness
Say everything to you of aliveness and mortality.

Celebrate the self that chimes, for
They are there with filled suitcases, Mom and Dad,
Looming in narrow doorways with you nevers and you forgots
                                          and how could yous
All, all true
All, all lies
And a Greek chorus of lovers, bearing witness.

Celebrate that self
And find in moments of a day's yearning
Or in the memory of a neglected dream
A cool mint tea of years and learning,
Sweet crumpled collage of frontier moments—
The best you could, the most you dared—
Jewels strung on a lace of days
Chiming in morning sunlight.

MILLENNIALS

For the Fire Circle Family

They're crying doom again, the priests
As the numbers conveniently round the calendar:
Sifting their auguries, seeing omens in the accumulation
Of small things. The Great Invisible Hand,
They say, is poised to smite us,
Call account for sudden payment
Of all accumulated sins.

This time, they've somewhat more
Than births of two-headed calves to go on
In their white coats, reading the future in the cupped
Spires of diminishing ice. Woe, we cry.

Around us, scrambling, people are their varied selves:
Slumping in defeat, angrily denying,
Bravely strategizing.

But we take a soft route: perhaps no less doomed
In the end, but kinder. The having of things pales before
The evening spent in shared truth, the meeting of moments
                                        that glow and ring.
We reach across the thorned thickets of our wary natures
To the only true thing we can find under the lowering sky:
Your eyes, mine, our hands held in wide circles whispering
Again and again I am here, you are not alone, we are here
                                                        together
Come what may, until the end of days.

FALLING THROUGH
For Selene

It seems as if
I'm always falling through you,
Reaching but not finding, like
Two ghosts repeating the movements,
Forgetting the words. There's shame
In the desperation of it:
The lungfuls of hair, the wanting
And trying too much, as if
Your tongue in my mouth could draw
The circle of that silver darkness
Again, as if
We had never come out into daylight, as
If the you I'd known still
Turns in slow grace, serene and perfect,
As if we could find each other again
That way, as if the moment isn't over,
As if I'd ever stop wanting you

THE VERY WORD

"Verse" I like: a friendly, earthy
Campfire familiar. But no, can't have that, not
With theses to write and small
-time books of criticism—
Nearly unintelligible—to say what the moment
Of a Stevens, a cummings meant:
Not verse.

Or "piece". Calm, technical, no chip
On the shoulder. Could be anything:
Sonata, jigsaw, Tinkertoy, transistor.
No great shakes. But no.

Instead, that other word, stark and effete
Arched across the broken diphthong like grinding gears,
No glide, just po-ehm, as they say it, a Grecian urn
And teacup sort of word for wimps,
For pansies,
And not the dark blood wonder of the thing
Cleaving language from itself until
              Splintered to wine and jazz it becomes

    All that language cannot

              Delivered by ragshod messenger
  (in secret code
          to)
                    the waiting heart

YEARS AFTER

You can see it if you look,
If you know how
To look: that hillock,
Green with years and
Intervening dirt. Entering the clearing,
This shape rises different, this
And half a worn, impassioned face
Protruding from the ground. It is here,
Hidden below.

We return here, again,
Again, for family outings:
Picnic lunch atop the stelae,
Conjecture how it must
Have been, wine and laughter,
A pleasant afternoon.

Below
Safe in civilizing darkness
Still the heat
Of ancient dances.

Wisely
We bring no shovels.

TROLL

That moment when the great clawed
Body of the garden spider heaves into view,
Stark and motionless,
Head down astride the thrown wheel of her artistry
Against the green chrysanthemums: horror
At the machined monster armor she arrays
There on a dew-wheel of morning,
Potent with the death she flexes,
Testing each strand and waiting,
As if I were small and niggling,
Chewing an ignorant leaf
And not looming here drawn and revolted,
Knowing whose garden it really is after all.

DEA GRATIAS

Open
Ever more open; arms flung wide
Let the warm, wet wings of your chest be spread until
Barehearted there
Only the longing of joy, of living is with you,
The sweetness of its unfolding generosity.
They are all there, the great and tiny miracles daily given,
A breath, a golden pebble, a scarlet cloud at sunset,
The voice of creation singing out to cold space, even which
—Even which—
Is life as well, out to blackness and beginnings all
Whirling and singing and spinning and changing
Omnipresent
The glory of the world in your heart's red petals there
Where first it placed a red kiss in your mother's womb
Saying Welcome.

Struggles and Sorrows

12/5/93: TAKING THE FLYER DOWN
For Polly Klaas

It's autumn, now, bright
And lovely melancholy for
A dying year. Today the fog
And drip obscure, mercifully
The irrevocable loss. There is
No turning back: the coming days are
Cold and dark.

In brighter days, this
Sheet declared: I reject evil,
I sustain hope.

The leaves are falling now,
Polly, like vanishing light,
Like
The death of innocence

DEPRESSION—a Cycle

HELLO

It's always been sideways and surfaces,
Looking for the best angle or focusing narrowly
On hair or the furrowing of skin, a conform to norm check
Or a tie that won't. Assessment, in its way
Reduced to parts; those green and gold eyes, how lucky,
Or damn it, how did you get so bald. Maintenance,
Not contemplation. Not often.

Now, knowing,
Having seen having walked the fog to stand
Beneath the lonely streetlight waiting
And memories channeling past like empty streetcars
Finished with defenses with excuses with contrition or abuse or
                                                                                                  contempt
Finished with the question of value, this:
You have to meet the eyes. There you are.

It's simple, it always was:
It's mental illness. The lens you train on the mirror
Lies.

It lies.

THE LIE

It's everywhere.
Emerging from the burrow from the cool wet changelessness
To rub against the world: it's in everything. And so, venturing out
There is a sort of panic dance, circling faster and faster
With fear clawing your lungs like a ferret in a bag
And rebounded from every wall, every eye, the lie:
No hope. No point. No joy. No future.

So run then: back to the pressed-close grave walls, the cool gray
                                                          motionless
                                                          solitude
Run to the movies to take an emotion from the library shelf: sorrow,
Or love. Run to the repeated and senseless motion of solitaire, a
                                                          hundred games,
A thousand deep
Into the night, and then morning breaking
And everywhere the lie, in everything, in the mew of the cat
Or the color of the bedclothes as the days become months, then years,
As the tiniest of tasks becomes Herculean, as the shower and razor
Are made Everest, or the moon
With the mouths of the loved moving but no sound coming out
As they grow baffled, then impatient and angry, the mouths going
                                                          faster
But there is no sound but the lie, thundering up from the ground
Ringing from the sky, welling like blood from the cracks in the world

And you know it's lying. You know.
But you can't help it. You listen.

TITRATION TWO-STEP

For all who have loved me. And Nemea, who saved me.

Titrate *(v): to add a reagent of known strength and measure the volume necessary to convert the constituent to another form. In pharmacology, to bring the concentration of an administered medication to a level of effectiveness.*

1. <u>Reeling</u>
It was a bad cocktail: bitter, and too thin.
It had always been wrong, but I had been served: it was my brain, and
I insisted I'd drink it. No chaser.

With time, the misproportion a dark wave across my eyes
I stumbled over what had seemed ordinary things,
Battered my arms blue in hopes of feeling, went maudlin
And enraged. The floor became the ceiling, then something like the
                                                                      moon,
Friends and furniture alike foreign, unnavigable. They gibbered
In the languages of stones about a somewhere physics of light
And seatedness, the alien topography of *calm, love, future*
Falling through me, touching nothing as I staggered, as I fell,
As my flailing elbows struck all that came near and the crowing only I
                                                                            could hear
Grew deafening: the triumph, the ecstasy of defeat.

This went on for some time.

I emptied my pockets on the floor
Lost everything
Scrambled as money and addresses and keys rolled beneath the
                                                                  Martian ottomans.

All eyes on me I said *I don't care this is how it ends*

But the burning in my chest said SHAME:
The last thing to go is the pretense of dignity.

Staring up at the forest of legs the stares and I wanted to reach for the
                                                                    hands
But struck at them
I wanted to pull my eyes out
I wanted I wanted but could not move
Until at last I lay silent, groping with numb clam hands
In tiny motions for useless things
And the cold rain began finally to fall, to end it.

I waited, relieved: no more trying. No more pride.

I never knew she was that strong, to get an arm under me like that
When my weight had grown so great I couldn't support it. To sit me up
And bring the one who had the pills, and make me swallow them
And sit with me, and wait.

I never knew until then
Though now it makes such sense
I was born drunk

2. Triage

I take pills to blunt the sting of it:
Stand tall, smile, make small talk and under
My clothes the blood is welling from the bandages, the blood
Of all my lost appendages
Taken in cruelty
Squandered with carelessness, worn to nubs
By the blowing grit of years of misdeeds,
Empty excuses stretched over failures again, again,
The proud standards I pimp but cannot live.
I see too much now, feel the blood running
Down the insides of my trousers
With their thrift-store tags and pride-sharp creases.
The mirror shows too much now, a thousand tinpot boasts
Disproven, the Great Man's swagger made
A stooped and graying shadow. Fallen away,
Appendages: the glib tongue spinning smart,
Lying. Blood pooling in my shoes and only the squelch
Of every step reminds me for here
In the Land of the Pills
I'd never know I was bleeding to death.

3. Here It Is

So here it is.
Today's sky is hard blue, announcing autumn.
The wan warm light antique with dust
Makes daguerrotypes of the country roads,
The trees against that unflinching blue,
No wind: a held stillness
At the peak of the arc before the fall.

There is no romance to it.
It's beautiful, but just a day, warm and pale,
Moving towards the end of the year. A perfume of oak leaves
Filled with memories, and the prospect of times ahead
Still growing in darkness,
The prospect of cold.

Something will happen,
Something between the dreaded and the dreamed.
Despair one voice only now,
Black certainty far away, a dream itself;
Possibility arriving late to the conversation
With unfamiliar news.

Not knowing—a new thing.
Swept nor numb.

Here it is: a day.

THE AVALANCHE

The avalanche took our home.

A wave of ice drove us before it,
And everything we thought we had we loaded on our backs
As we fled, but no luck: the cold fist ground us under.
Home. Years. Love. Work. Health.
We cried as it passed over us, scraping,
Pinned in place, locked in dim blue light:
Frozen.

The avalanche took our hope.

We lay motionless, pockets collapsing about us
Stripping away more and more, and we did nothing:
Only gazed upward, and mourned, and remembered
And night came, and all disappeared
But a smear of muted stars.

And it wasn't until the sun returned, and murky light
Bathed us in the how and where we were
A sprout insisted beneath my hand.

I got an arm free, and reached. Scraped. Swam.
And when we emerged with our poor remnants and our lives
The white expanse was dotted with green:
Life indomitable, pressing into morning light.

VARICELLA
Chicken pox at 40: a voyage

Varicella: lovely name, a charmer
she whirls me away from my life, leading through unfamiliar steps
shaking with longing, filled with fever dreams and Varicella
whispering in my ears she says *Mark sweet take a ride*
Do you see what I can do for you
and I can't swallow can't drink my thirst is all
for Varicella, tapping out runes on my back and arms
a riot of who would believe. Taken like a lover
like food
spinning her way across my face Varicella says,
Nightmare now. No sleep.
and so I stare into the night, ears filling with Varicella
wondering how I lasted so long without her, hating her,
knowing she was always mine and coming until
the fever breaks again and her tattoo across my chest
is leopard spots and Maori initiations, Varicella whispering
as she runs down the dark corridors of my blood
I have a secret, and I wait for it, the fever again
but she is leaving now, curling into herself to make
a warm nest of nerves. She is almost gone, leaving her mess when
she says one more thing. *Mark*, she says, *all these Marks will fade*

and then all you were denied in childhood will be yours.

I have been waiting to bring you these gifts. Do not hate me
so much, says Varicella

and then she is gone.

The Wheel of the Year

MULLED WINE (Yule)

It begins where the smoke
Hits your eyes: smouldering peat,
Mutton stew on a broad iron hook,
Deep snow: How can it ever
Have been summer? Apples wrinkling
And mice in the barley—
With so much to fear, thank fortune
For company! We'll tell our tales,
Remember how we passed the cold
Last year, and last, and those
Who couldn't. The grape leans across
The seasons, clasps the hand of summer's
Dried rind, dreaming the new fruit,
Calling the sun back, world
Without end,
Amen.

THREE PERCENT (Brightening/Imbolc)

Three percent is all they say
The sweet water of a water planet

Three percent
The cool drink, the soft rain
Rare as blood, rare as luck, rare
To our wet hands, shining.
From the far sky, adrift in curds and blankets
Whips and knots, anvils towering thunder hammers
Rain the hand of kindness down
To our fields, our mouths, the dancing springs
And cold rivers, snaking the glens of Earth to the sky again.
Do we take you for granted, o three percent?
Do we curse you for flooding, pop our grumbrellas
On a wet walk to the office?

Not I.

Not when puddles leap for joy and silver makes the sky
A treasury. I tip my face to you, and appearances be damned
This gift is too precious: oceans' breath, sky's milk
Rivers' song falling drop by drop
To my waiting skin.

SPRING LAUGHS (High Spring)

It begins with a giggle:
The tiniest white tendril reaching from the secret soil
Like a child's laugh, the purr of a cat and then
Raising, greening leaves and flowers peal across the meadows,
Carpet even what was once severe, sere,
Frowning brown in summer's dry thatch,
A deep belly rumble of soaring chlorophyll
Spreading wanton leaves, dangling perfumed sex
Climbing to nod and wave come and get me,
These meadows,
Brazen to the skip of children gathering posies
Bees lumbering slow in the crisp morning air
You, and I, perhaps, gone down to the stream
To lay down in that place, screened by waving rye
And the laughter of the stream gurgling out like a baby's delight
Playing with our playthings as we do, exploring
The whole world green and gripped with the howl of it:
Spring come at last.

MAY MORNING (May Day)

Fresh as the day the world was made,
This morning: dew-spattered through feather fans
Of foxtail and wild rye. Still as a caught breath, the day, hushed,
Holds for a slow-golding time, the rose hints
Of bold and bright to come, of music
Yet to be made, dances old as the village, new as tomorrow's
                                                      milk.
How can it be, four billion, five hundred million years, the old
                                                    and battered Earth,
Veteran of ice and fire, meteor, petroleum, stupidity, avarice,
                                                        ignorance
How can it be, this innocence: rye tops waving hello, good
                                                     morning,
Beads of crystal dew filled with beauty wash,
The bright face of the Golden One coming,
Bringing suit to his blue lover again,
And Earth meeting him with an armload of flowers
As if all the grief were undone, as if
(As it is)
The sorrows and losses don't matter, really,
Not in the face of this coming morning
When Earth says Yes
Sun says I Am Here
The great rounding of things stately in its time,
The lone bird calling to a lightening sky
He is risen
He is risen

DAWN PRAYER (Midsummer)

Whose warm love flows across the land each day
Stirring Life, the world's magic, arms yearning up,
Turning each green leaf to follow. Whose generous balm
Upon the skin is love's touch, *ahhhhhh* heated fingers soothing,
Whose roar boils water from ocean to sky
Drawing sweet from salt, becoming rain, snow, river, lake;
Whose fervid beat upon us is deadly, and yet
Contemplating cold stars how we miss it,
The Golden One, quotidian center
Of our days, steady companion, sower of treasures great and
                                                        small:
Light-bringer, Life-quickener, dazzling, unbearably bright,
Hail, oh hail the magnificent Sun!

GIFTS OF A PROBLEM SABBATH (Dimming)

Hidden, you spring upon us from the calendar: ah!
The Marblemouthed Holiday is upon us again!
What shall we call it? Lammas, or Lughnasadh how on Earth
Do you pronounce that, but worse, what does it mean?

Behold the midpoint, the blazing furnace of August.
Ritual? Indoors, perhaps, but not under that Sun.

Rather, let us go to the places of water to bask,
To where berries hang heavy among the thorns,
Knowing it all starts now the cascade of food pouring
From the good Earth. Break
A stalk of barley, saying *this is my heritage* this
Is emmer wheat is einkorn is the tough grass of the Fertile
                                              Crescent
Bred to bake my loaves. And bake one then, a crusty yeasty
                                              rosemary
Dome for tearing with the hands. Eat warm with butter or oil,
Feel the Life milling in your teeth, and swallow:
This good life sprung abundant from the collision of Earth's
                                              magic,
Time and art and science. We are a making people. Our hoes and
                                              lore
Midwife the coming of apples and squash, peppers, tomatoes.
The Great Gathering begins now.

THE CRUSH (Harvest)

Stain the air purple, grape!
Seethe in the warmth of September,
Plucked in ripe clusters and driven the dusty vineyard row.
Swathe us round with the smell of sweating ferment
In these long golden days. Tease us with the hint
Of next year's vintage:
Tell us secrets of the future.

Fall, round apple!
Weigh the lichened boughs to breaking,
Filled with memory: white flowers and wassail milk
The crabbed dance of the winter orchard.
In the spiced warm of September. delight us with pie
And crumble, sauce and butter, cider hard and soft:
Speak the secret of the past.

Swell, ripe pumpkin!
Hide a nestled treasure in the vine, glowing,
Brain a mess of seeds and strings
Awaiting eyes and mouth for Hallows.
Fill the pies and carry the spice
Hinting winter, whispering snow
Say the words: the fleeting now.

IN MEMORIAM SOLIS VICTI (Autumn)

He grows old, whose fingers dancing on my face
Once left their fiery prints there, whose great wide roar
Brought all to cowering retreat beneath the cudgel of his heat—
He grows old. His head bows wan, white
As faded bunting, shuffling to the basement where lay stored
His youth's memories.

She prepares a place for him, in earth browned by his passing,
And smears her face with his blood. The flakes drop
One, then another, leaving bones and cold wind.

She weaves a green dress for the service, one struggled strand at
                                                             a time.

She will weep all through the winter, labor alone in the dark,
His progeny's pale head peering out to grow.

MYSTERY (Hallows)

For Pat and Jeff Winters, in memory of their son

I. Wail

Encompass this: as an egg snake
Swallowing a jagged, broken stone would unhinge,
Unhinge and stretch
But cannot swallow without blood and scar.
Stretch your mouth until the howl is your dark heart's blood
Poured on the floor of the world.
Tear the words from the walls of your body:
Never. Never. Forever.

II. Dark Road

Without notice, he turned from us,
Not a backward glance, and lit a lantern to walk
Into that dark country. We could see his light awhile.
It grew far and faint, then gone. We followed seven steps,
As far as bloodwarmed feet could take us. Time changed.

Nothing mattered.

Dust became the clotting of everything, and the sweet
Temple scent of myrrh, lavender, lotus, the dimness
Of candleglow became a comfort:
Easier to stay, lay the long bones down,
Light a lantern, walk the dark road too.

III. Pulse

The world's insistence thrums in the body
And denies surrender: the mouth craves food,
The ear speech, the eye color. My loves,
Yet living,
Called me to set the long pendulum swinging again,
To retrace my steps from the dark:
One, another.
A month from now, perhaps two more.

The seventh, though, will never return.
One foot, informed,
Remains upon the track he left
When first he turned his face from us.

IV. Grace

In the stark room at her center—
The innermost coffin, alabaster still,
Without which howl the ten thousand bereftitudes—
In that most private chamber comes a grace
That is the knowing of what must be.

Here no wars are fought with what is.
Here there is only knowledge.

She finds her love there, opens her hands,
Knowing what must be done.

V. Hole

And so it is seen, gazing down to the bottom
Of that forever hole, that our world,
Seeming so substantial, is yet hollow, a crust
Thin and fragile and subject to sinkhole
Without notice or reason. The hollow world holds us,
A bubble of clay above the falling darkness whose mouth
We mark with stones and flowers.

In the bottom is a dark mirror. Dimly, through a smoke
Gaze of averted eyes and cobbled tales we speak
To ease the awful finality of it, comes a face: mine.
Yours. All of ours, all we love, in time:
And not much of it. To look down where the flowers,
Where the swathed limbs make the shape of living
And yet are not, will never live again
Is the seen truth, the known pattern of all precious and guarded
                                                                things.

VI. Kyrie

O dark and odious inscrutable Force
Whose disembodied Name we cannot know, but fear:
Hear me.

My pious acceptances are a tissue of flimsy thoughts.
I hate and fear You utterly.

I plead, though you give no thought to mercy,
For mercy.

I pray, though You show no sign of kindness,
For kindness.

VIGIL

Winter stands in the corner of my garden,
Rounds her shoulders, tucks her chin, draws tight her cloak of
                                                                   stars and ice,
Razor moon and rain. Spare and erect, gaunt in the darkness,
Bark-peeling with moss predation, slick and black she nods,
She waits, she leans,

The sky shows her jewelry, vents its wet moods. Death litters
The paths with bones and brown rags. Secret life skulks then like
                                                                    a thief:
She finds mushrooms between her toes, grows green and furry
                                                                     slippers.

Long, long.

Until one day the clearwashed air grows sweet and yellow
With acacia, and her memory stirs with the taste
Of a near-forgotten lover's scent, feels again the warmth of his
                                                                     regard,
Stretches,
Stretches to find him again,
Turning up her daffodil face.

ABOUT THE AUTHOR

Mark A. Green is an activist, writer, poet, musician and lover of the Earth. Founding Executive Director of Sonoma County Conservation Action, he developed the organization into the largest environmental group on the North Coast of California, for which he was recognized by Congress and the California Legislature, and named Sonoma County Environmentalist of the Year.

He is the author of *Atheopaganism, an Earth-Honoring Path Rooted in Science*, which describes a spirituality of critical thinking, reverence, joy and exploration. His writing appears at Atheopaganism.org and several other online forums.

He lives with the delightful Nemea on occupied lands of the Southern Pomo and Coast Miwok peoples, in the watershed of the Russian River.

www.ingramcontent.com/pod-product-compliance
Lightning Source LLC
Chambersburg PA
CBHW051412290426
44108CB00015B/2257